Published by Smart Apple Media,
an imprint of Black Rabbit Books
P.O. Box 3263, Mankato, Minnesota 56002
www.blackrabbitbooks.com

Published by arrangement with
The Salariya Book Company Ltd

Cataloging-in-Publication Data is available
from the Library of Congress

Printed in the United States
At Corporate Graphics,
North Mankato, Minnesota

9 8 7 6 5 4 3 2 1

ISBN: 978-1-62588-338-4

Illustrators: Nicholas Hewetson
David Antram

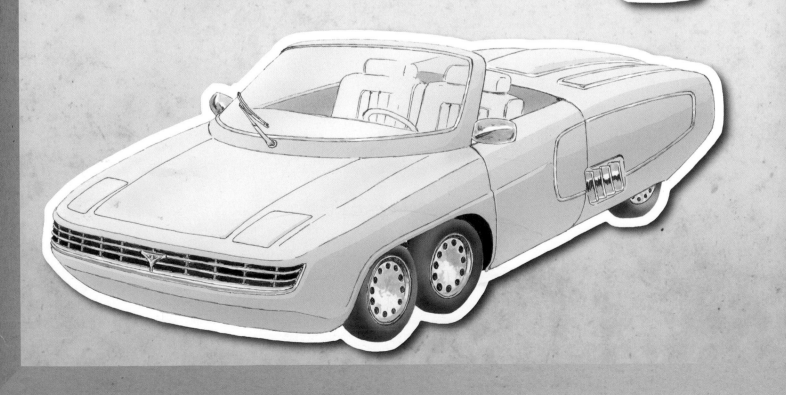

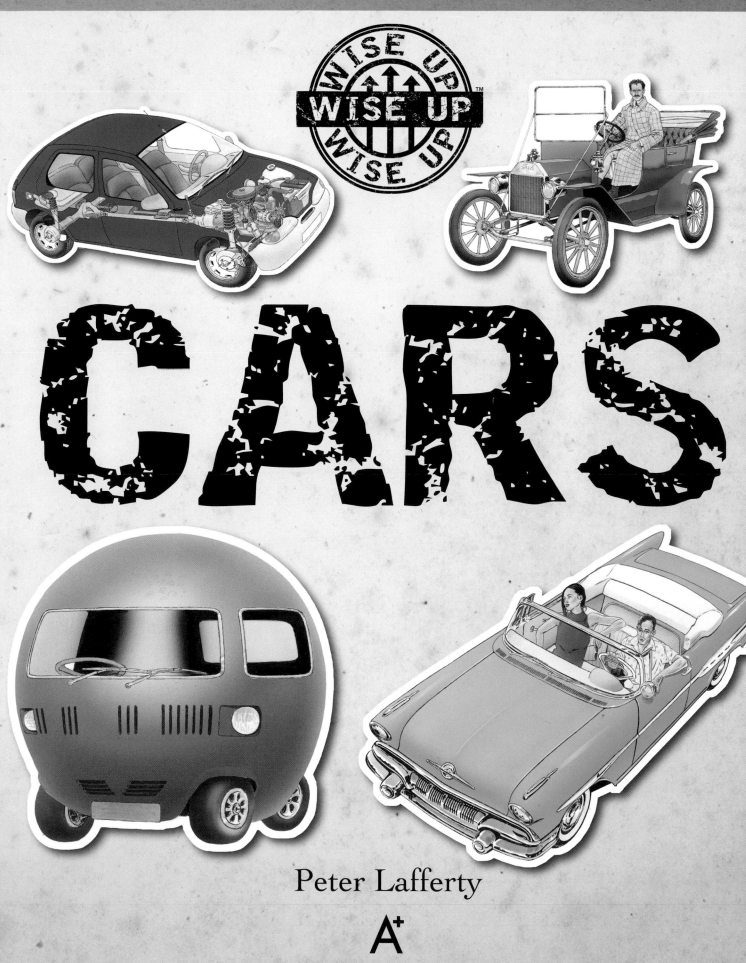

CARS

Peter Lafferty

A+

Smart Apple Media

Contents

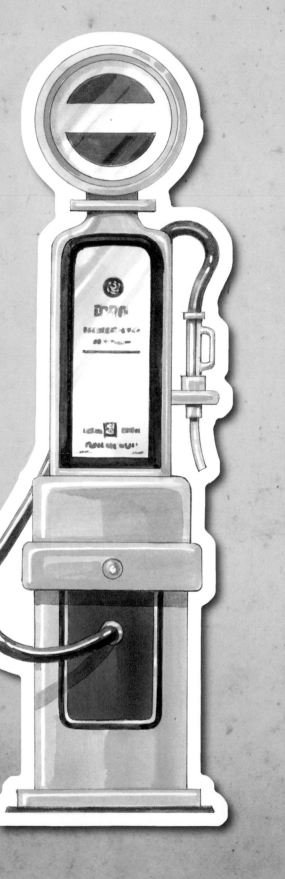

The Age of Cars

Car Designers

▼ New cars are designed on computers. Different body shapes and color schemes can be quickly visualized on screen.

Car Factory

▲ To keep up with the demand, millions of cars are made each year. Germany alone produces 110,000 cars every week—that's 5.7 million new cars a year.

FACTFILE
DOUBLE THE NUMBER
In 2010 there were more than 1 billion cars in the world. By 2030, experts think there will be 2 billion, and China will have more than any other country.

The motor car is part of modern life and is used for business and pleasure. However, while cars have changed the lives of many people, they have also brought problems. In some cities, there are now so many cars on the roads that traffic can be slower than in the days of the horse-drawn cart, and it frequently grinds to a halt. The car has also brought pollution to the streets.

▶ Racing cars provide an exciting sport for both drivers and spectators.

▲ The fastest Formula 1 racers reach speeds of over 220 mph (360 km/h).

▲ For some people a car is essential. Doctors must travel to patients' homes at any time of the day or night. They may need to reach remote farms and villages.

◀ Many people drive to the mountains or seaside for their holidays. Cars allow them to tour around to see the local sights.

▲ Cars with six or more seats are ideal for large families.

FACTFILE
CARS ON THE ROAD

In 2011, the countries with the most cars per 1,000 people were:

- San Marino: 1,263
- Monaco: 842
- Liechtenstein: 826
- United States: 809
- Iceland: 747
- Luxembourg: 741.

Traffic Jams

▼ In 2013, a traffic jam stretched for 192 miles (309 km) on roads around São Paulo, Brazil. In 2010, on the China National Highway, cars were trapped in a 62-mile (99-km) traffic jam for 12 days.

The First Cars

The first motor cars were powered by large steam engines which were not suitable for small road vehicles. In 1876, a smaller four-stroke engine was invented by German engineer Nikolaus August Otto. The first vehicle to use a four-stroke gasoline engine, the Motorwagen, took to the roads in 1885. It was built by Karl Benz in Mannheim, Germany. Early motor cars looked like horse-drawn carriages and were called "horseless carriages."

▼ Captain Nicolas-Joseph Cugnot, of the French Artillery Corps, made the first practical self-propelled vehicle. It was powered by a steam engine and took to the road in 1769. Unfortunately, it crashed into a wall on its first journey—the world's first motor vehicle accident.

FACTFILE
CHEAP MOTORING

In 1904 it was cheaper to run a car than a carriage. An Oldsmobile car cost only $600. Even with the cost of gasoline, oil, and repairs, this still only came to about two-thirds the price of feeding and stabling a pair of horses.

Karl Benz's Motorwagen was a three-wheeler, with a top speed of 12 mph (20 km/h). Benz went on to found a famous car-making firm.

◄ The first four-wheeled car was built by another German, Gottlieb Daimler, in 1886. The car used a four-stroke gasoline engine.

▲ Early cars upset horses and people as they sped past. Motorists were often called "cads on wheels."

FACTFILE
MOTORING FIRSTS
- First successful steam-powered car: England, 1803.
- First steam vehicle to travel over 93 miles (150 km) without breaking down: England, 1840.
- First traffic signals: England, 1868.
- First car license plates: France, 1893.

Gasoline Pump

▲ The first gasoline pump appeared in the United States in 1906. Before this, motorists had to buy their fuel from the local pharmacy or drugstore.

▼ Early motorists wore goggles, hats, and thick clothing to keep out the cold and dust. This is a 1913 Napier.

Ford Model T

▲ The Ford Model T was the first mass-produced motor car. It was called "the people's car" because it was the first car that ordinary people could afford. It was produced from 1908 to 1927. Over 16 million Model T cars were made.

▼ Dragsters are designed to produce maximum acceleration from a standing start on a straight track. They can reach speeds of 330 mph (530 km/h).

Dragster

Types of Car

There are many different types of car, each designed for a particular use. A family car is designed to accommodate the whole family. It usually does not need a very powerful engine. A sports car is often a two-seater but has a powerful engine. A racing car seats only the driver, but it has an even more powerful engine that can only be used for high-speed racing. Family cars perform many tasks.

▲ Cars known as 'people carriers' are popular for short city journeys.

▲ Off-road vehicles often have a powerful winch to pull the vehicle out of mud.

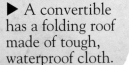

► A convertible has a folding roof made of tough, waterproof cloth.

► A luxury sports car combines speed with a stylish appearance. The engine and gearbox take up much of the interior.

▶ Racing cars have flaps called airfoils at the front and back. Air rushing over them forces the car down, improving its grip on the track.

Racing Car

▲ Rally driving is a sport in which cars race across country. The cars are often ordinary road vehicles.

◀ A dune buggy has wide tires to stop it sinking into the sand, and roll bars to protect the driver if the buggy topples.

▲ Go-carts or karts are very small, specially built cars which race around a track.

▲ Off-road vehicles are built for driving across country without tarmacked roads. They have four-wheel drive, which transmits engine power to each wheel.

How a Car Works

 motor car is made up of around 30,000 different parts which must all work in harmony. These parts are arranged into several different "systems," each performing one major task. The transmission system transmits the engine's power to the wheels. The fuel system ensures that the engine gets the fuel it needs, while the electrical system provides the electricity needed. Other systems allow the car to be steered, slowed down, and stopped, and ensure a comfortable ride.

FACTFILE
MOTOR FIRSTS
- First differential gear: France, 1828.
- First air-filled car tire: France, 1895.
- First electric starter motor: England, 1896.
- First honeycomb radiator: Germany, 1898.

propeller shaft

wheel

tire

differential

muffler

exhaust pipe

▲ The transmission system transmits the power of the engine to the wheels by a series of shafts. The gearbox alters the speed at which the engine turns the wheels. The differential stops the wheels from skidding when the car turns.

◄ Gasoline is pumped to the engine by the fuel pump. Before entering the engine, the gasoline is turned into a gas that is mixed with air. This happens in the carburettor.

▼ The body shell is the metal frame on which most parts of the car are fixed.

▲ The body shell is reinforced with steel bars to protect the passengers.

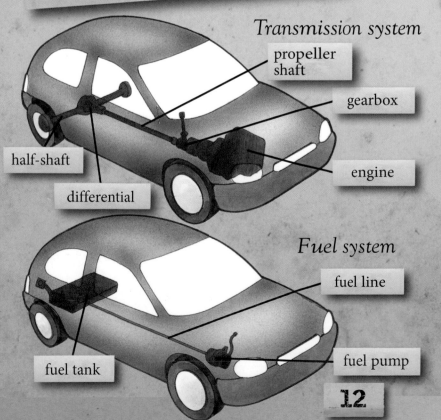

Transmission system

propeller shaft

gearbox

engine

half-shaft

differential

Fuel system

fuel line

fuel tank

fuel pump

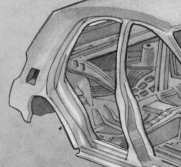

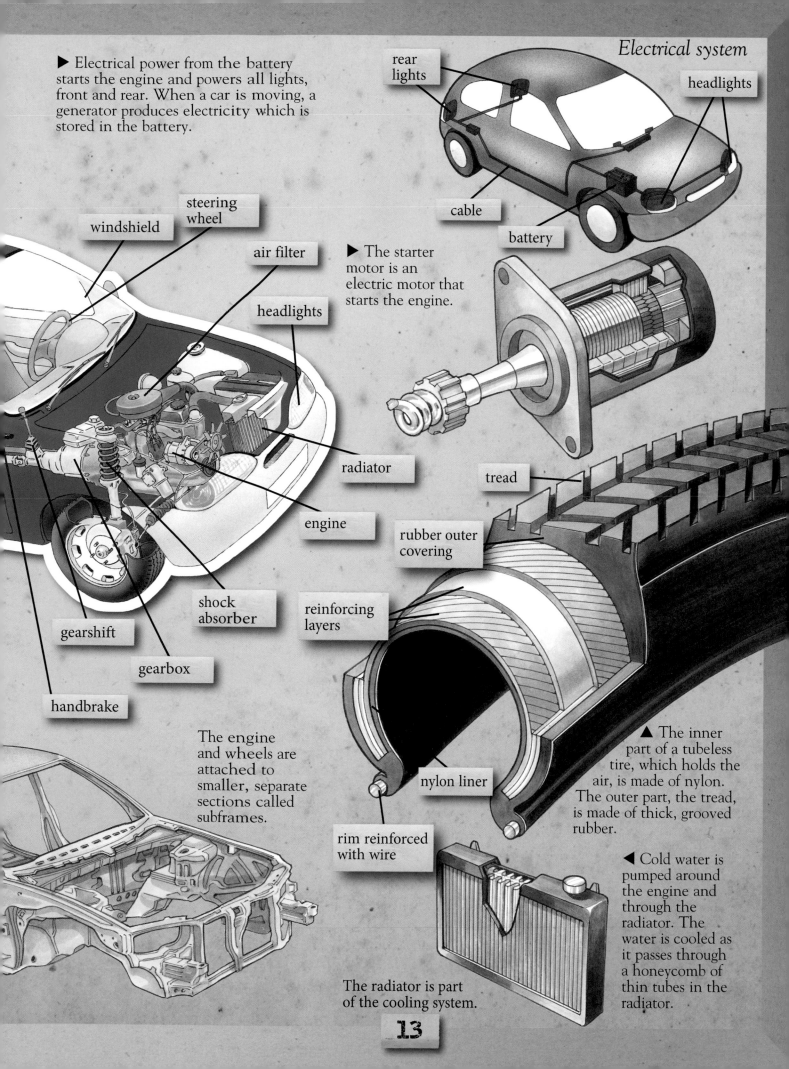

▶ Electrical power from the battery starts the engine and powers all lights, front and rear. When a car is moving, a generator produces electricity which is stored in the battery.

Electrical system

rear lights

headlights

cable

battery

windshield

steering wheel

air filter

headlights

▶ The starter motor is an electric motor that starts the engine.

radiator

tread

engine

rubber outer covering

reinforcing layers

shock absorber

gearshift

gearbox

handbrake

nylon liner

rim reinforced with wire

The engine and wheels are attached to smaller, separate sections called subframes.

▲ The inner part of a tubeless tire, which holds the air, is made of nylon. The outer part, the tread, is made of thick, grooved rubber.

◀ Cold water is pumped around the engine and through the radiator. The water is cooled as it passes through a honeycomb of thin tubes in the radiator.

The radiator is part of the cooling system.

13

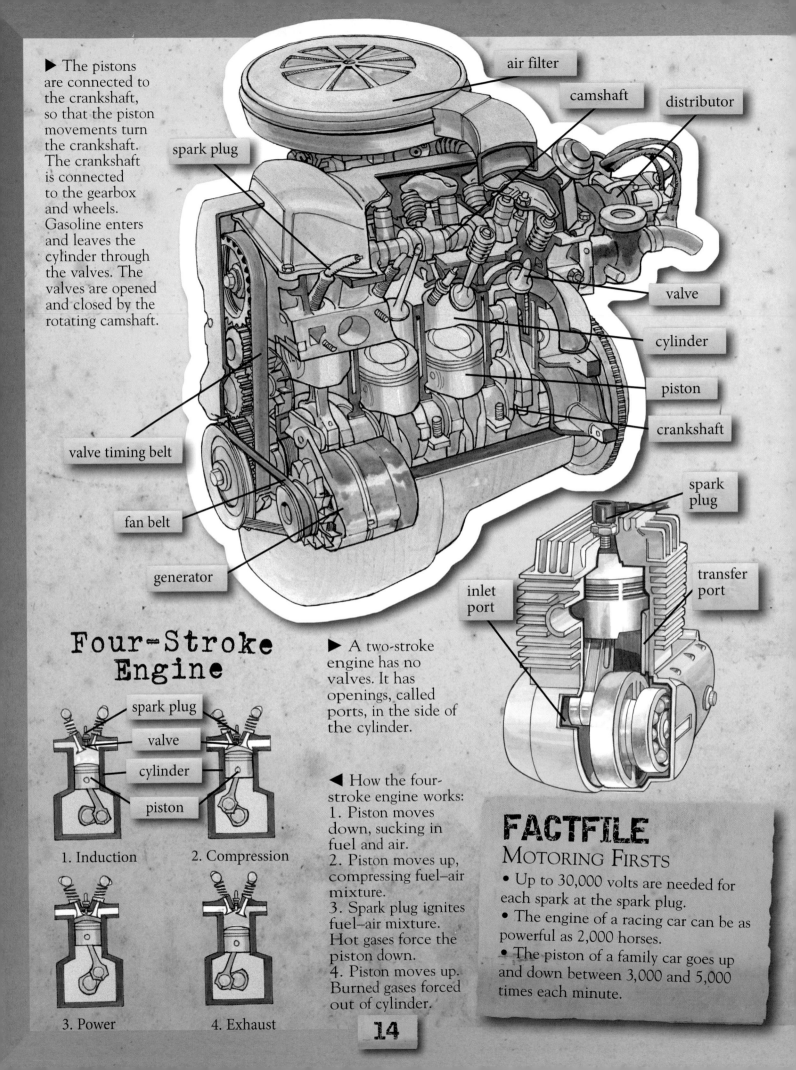

► The pistons are connected to the crankshaft, so that the piston movements turn the crankshaft. The crankshaft is connected to the gearbox and wheels. Gasoline enters and leaves the cylinder through the valves. The valves are opened and closed by the rotating camshaft.

air filter

camshaft

distributor

spark plug

valve

cylinder

piston

crankshaft

spark plug

transfer port

inlet port

valve timing belt

fan belt

generator

Four-Stroke Engine

spark plug

valve

cylinder

piston

1. Induction

2. Compression

3. Power

4. Exhaust

► A two-stroke engine has no valves. It has openings, called ports, in the side of the cylinder.

◄ How the four-stroke engine works:
1. Piston moves down, sucking in fuel and air.
2. Piston moves up, compressing fuel–air mixture.
3. Spark plug ignites fuel–air mixture. Hot gases force the piston down.
4. Piston moves up. Burned gases forced out of cylinder.

FACTFILE
MOTORING FIRSTS
• Up to 30,000 volts are needed for each spark at the spark plug.
• The engine of a racing car can be as powerful as 2,000 horses.
• The piston of a family car goes up and down between 3,000 and 5,000 times each minute.

Driving Force

 gasoline engine is sometimes called an "internal combustion engine," because gasoline is burned inside it. Gasoline, an energy-rich liquid produced from crude oil, is burned inside a metal tube called a cylinder. This causes a piston to move up and down inside the cylinder. Each movement is called a stroke. Most motor cars have a four-stroke engine, which produces power with four movements of the piston. Motorcycles, and some small cars, have two-stroke engines.

▲ Four cylinders create a smoother ride since one of the cylinders is producing power at any one time.

FACTFILE
ENGINE POSITION

The engine and the driving wheels can be arranged in several ways:
1. engine at front, rear wheel drive;
2. engine in middle, rear wheel drive;
3. engine at rear, rear wheel drive;
4. engine at front, front wheel drive.

Carburettor

▶ A carburettor mixes air with a fine spray of gasoline. This mixture flows into the cylinder.

▶ In a diesel engine, a spark plug is not normally needed. However, when the engine is first started the air must be warmed by the preheater.

Diesel preheater

◀ A spark jumps across the gap at the bottom of the spark plug, between outer and central electrodes. A high-voltage cable is connected to the top of the plug.

spark gap

A driver needs to be able to steer and to stop the car, so two important systems take care of these needs. The steering system allows the driver to move in all directions, and the braking system allows the driver to stop the car. The suspension system makes a journey much more comfortable. It consists of springs and shock absorbers under the car. These stop the car from bouncing too much on bumpy roads.

▲ These leaf springs were used in the suspension systems of early cars.

▶ In four-wheel steering, both front and rear wheels turn. For easy parking, front and rear wheels turn in opposite directions. At high speeds, front and rear wheels turn in the same direction.

Steering

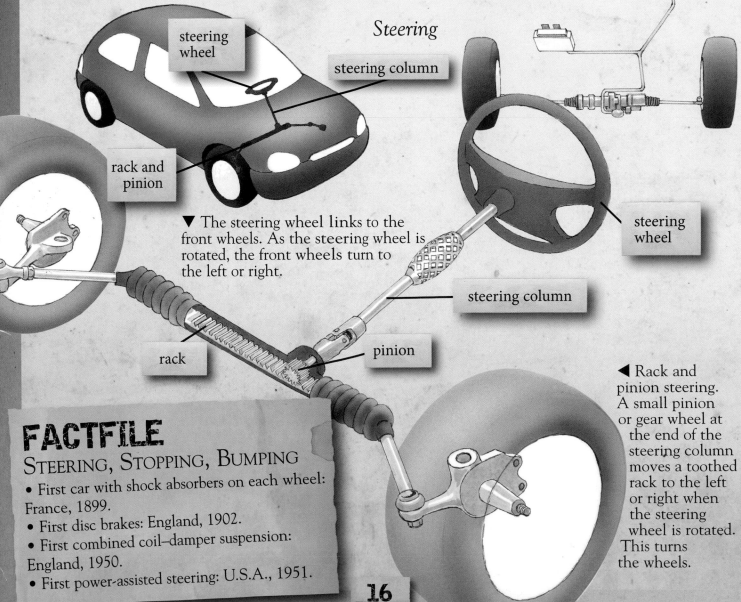

steering wheel

steering column

rack and pinion

steering wheel

steering column

▼ The steering wheel links to the front wheels. As the steering wheel is rotated, the front wheels turn to the left or right.

pinion

rack

◀ Rack and pinion steering. A small pinion or gear wheel at the end of the steering column moves a toothed rack to the left or right when the steering wheel is rotated. This turns the wheels.

FACTFILE
STEERING, STOPPING, BUMPING
• First car with shock absorbers on each wheel: France, 1899.
• First disc brakes: England, 1902.
• First combined coil–damper suspension: England, 1950.
• First power-assisted steering: U.S.A., 1951.

▼ Leaf springs are still used in the suspension systems of trucks and buses.

springy metal strips

▼ A shock absorber consists of a strong coiled spring that allows the wheels to move up and down, and a damper that prevents the car from bouncing too much over bumps.

damper

shock absorbers

coil spring

Suspension

▲ The suspension system consists of shock absorbers located near each wheel. Each shock absorber is bolted to a strengthened area of the body shell and fixed to the subframe, to which the wheels are attached.

Brakes

brake pedal

◄ The braking system. Pipes full of oil connect the brake pedal to the brakes on each wheel. When the pedal is pushed, the pressure produced in the oil forces a pad against a drum or disc attached to each wheel.

▲ Disc brakes are usually fitted to the front wheels of a car. They are more powerful than drum brakes, which are usually fitted to the rear wheels.

drum brake

brake pipe

disc brake

FACTFILE
EMERGENCY STOP

The brief period between a driver seeing danger and applying the brakes is called the thinking distance. The braking distance is the distance traveled before a braked car finally comes to a standstill.

19.5 feet (6 m) + 19.5 feet (6 m)
at 20 mph (32 km/h)

40 feet (12 m) + 80 feet (24 m)
at 40 mph (64 km/h)

59 feet (18 m) + 180 feet (54 m)
at 60 mph (96 km/h)

Thinking distance ■ Braking distance

◀ In 1899, in France, an electric car called *La Jamais Contente* broke the world speed record. It reached a speed of 65 mph (106 km/h).

Speed Records

batteries

gasoline engine

batteries

◀ A modern hybrid electric car has a gasoline engine for use on long journeys and an electric motor for short journeys. The batteries for the electric motor are recharged when the gasoline engine is being used.

▶ Photocells produce an electric current when light falls on them. Many cells must be connected together to produce enough electricity to drive a car.

◀ An electric motor. The central part, called the rotor, consists of coils of wire, and rotates when electricity flows through the coils. The outer part, the stator, does not move.

stator

rotor

FACTFILE
POWERED DIFFERENTLY

In 1912, there was a mixture of cars on the road:
- 40% of cars were steam-powered.
- 38% of cars used electric batteries.
- 22% of cars used gasoline engines.

Different Power

A steam car called *The Rocket* broke the land speed record in Florida in 1906. It reached a speed of 121 mph (195 km/h).

The earliest cars were powered by steam engines or electric batteries. In 1911, the electric starter motor was invented, which meant that a gasoline car could be started quickly—a steam car took much longer to get going. Gasoline cars could also fill up with fuel faster than a steam car. An electric car needed frequent stops to recharge, so the gasoline car soon became the most popular type of car. Today, electric cars are making a comeback because they create less pollution.

In 1979 in California, American Stan Barrett drove a rocket-powered car faster than the speed of sound. His three-wheeled car, *Budweiser Rocket*, reached a speed of 739 mph (1,190 km/h).

FACTFILE
DOG POWER

In the 1880s, a car powered by dogs took to the roads in France. Invented by a Monsieur Huret, the car's rear wheels were large treadmills in which dogs ran to keep the car moving.

oxygen tank

fuel tank

pump

combustion chamber

In a rocket engine, the hot exhaust gases that blast out of the combustion chamber push the rocket forward.

88

Each year, electric cars powered by photocells on their roofs and sides race across Australia from Darwin to Adelaide, a distance of 1,864 miles (3,021 km), in about six days.

Motorists must obey traffic laws. For example, they must not exceed speed limits and must stop or slow down as required at road junctions. Car manufacturers now install seat belts and air bags in cars, and build car bodies that offer more protection for passengers in a crash. Braking systems have also been improved.

GIVE WAY

◀ Traffic signs indicate the rules of the road and inform motorists of imminent changes in road conditions.

side-impact bars

Ford

10%

▼ On high-speed roads, traffic signs indicate the speed limit, or give information about road conditions. Electronic signs can be updated as driving conditions change.

◀ Crash dummies used to test seat belts look just like people but contain instruments to measure the effects of a crash on the human body.

▶ The front of a car is designed to crumple in a head-on collision. This reduces the force of impact so passengers are thrown forward less violently.

FACTFILE
FLYING THE FLAG

In 1865, a law was introduced in Britain which required every powered road vehicle to have three drivers: one to steer, one to keep the engine going, and one to walk ahead waving a red flag to warn other traffic. The speed limit was 4 mph (6.4 km/h) in the country, and 2 mph (3.2 km/h) in towns.

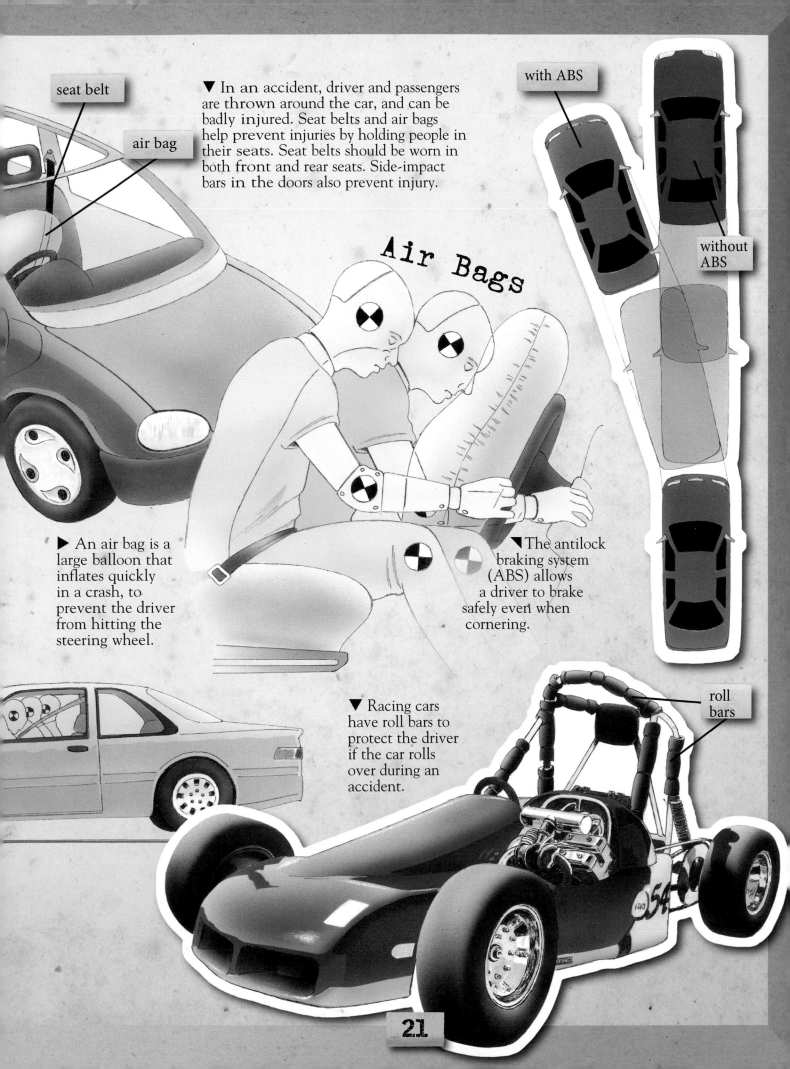

seat belt

air bag

▼ In an accident, driver and passengers are thrown around the car, and can be badly injured. Seat belts and air bags help prevent injuries by holding people in their seats. Seat belts should be worn in both front and rear seats. Side-impact bars in the doors also prevent injury.

with ABS

without ABS

Air Bags

▶ An air bag is a large balloon that inflates quickly in a crash, to prevent the driver from hitting the steering wheel.

▼ The antilock braking system (ABS) allows a driver to brake safely even when cornering.

roll bars

▼ Racing cars have roll bars to protect the driver if the car rolls over during an accident.

21

Weird Cars

Strange vehicles seen on the roads have included a motorized baby carriage, made in 1922, with a platform for a nurse to ride on, and the Vultee aerocar of 1947, which had detachable wings, enabling it to fly. The Red Bug Buckboard was the cheapest car ever made, costing only $125 in 1922. It was made mainly from bicycle parts. It had wooden seats, no roof or side panels, and a very feeble motor.

▲ This car was made for a publicity stunt. The fiberglass orange was attached to a small car called the Mini.

▼ The Leyat Aerocar was built in France in the 1920s. It was pulled along by a large propeller, and reached a speed of 100 mph (160 km/h).

▲The Panther 6 of 1977 had four front wheels to reduce the risk of skidding on wet roads. It was expected to reach speeds of 200 mph (320 km/h).

Leyat Aerocar

▲ In the 1970s, Malcolm Buchanan drove across the Irish Sea from the Isle of Man to England in a Volkswagen Beetle fitted with a propeller.

► American astronauts on the Moon in the 1970s used a collapsible vehicle called the Moon buggy. Powered by electric batteries, it could reach speeds of 10 mph (16 km/h).

FACTFILE
SPEEDING ON THE MOON

An unmanned Moon buggy from the *Apollo 16* mission holds two records. It reached a speed of 11 mph (18 km/h) when going downhill, and it traveled the greatest distance on the Moon: 21 miles (34 km).

◄ The 1957 Mercedes 300SL had "gull wing" doors which opened upward. A few modern cars still use these, although they are more difficult to close than normal doors.

▼ The 1950s "bubble car" was popular with city motorists. It was small enough to fit front-first into a parking space. The driver stepped out of a door at the front of the car.

The Beast

▼ This bulletproof Lincoln Continental Executive was made for the President of the United States. Since 2009, the President has used a Cadillac nicknamed "The Beast."

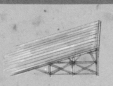

Record Breakers

▲ In 1983, Jacqueline De Creed jumped her Ford Mustang a distance of 229 feet (70 m) between two ramps.

In 1997 a jet-powered car called *Thrust* SSC smashed the world land speed record. It streaked across the Nevada desert at faster than the speed of sound, reaching 766.6 mph (1,233.7 km/h). A go-cart has been driven 1,056 miles (1,700 km) in 24 hours, and one Volkswagen Beetle has traveled a distance of 1,442,022 miles (2,320,745 km)—these are a few of the many motoring records that have been set.

◄ Inside a jet engine, fuel is burned in the combustion chamber. Hot exhaust gases that blast from the rear of the engine push the engine forward.

FACTFILE
FASTEST PRODUCTION CARS
• Bugatti Veyron Super Sport, 268 mph (431 km/h)
• Hennessey Venom GT, 266 mph (428 km/h)
• Koenigsegg Agera R, 260 mph (418 km/h)
• Bugatti Veyron Grand Sport Vitesse, 254 mph (409 km/h)
• Zenvo ST1, 233 mph (375 km/h)

FACTFILE
BEST-SELLING CARS
• Toyota Corolla: 40,000,000 sold since 1966.
• Volkswagen Beetle: 21,529,464 sold since 1937.
• VAZ 2100 (Lada 1200): 19,300,000 vehicles sold since 1970.
• Ford Model T: 16,536,075 vehicles sold since 1908.

► In 1930, Charles Creighton and James Hargis drove a Model A Ford in reverse from New York to Los Angeles and back, a distance of 7,180 miles (11,555 km).

Los Angeles

▲ An attempt on the land speed record in 1908. Algernon Guinness drove his 8-cylinder Darracq across Saltburn Sands, England, at 118 mph (190 km/h).

▶ The longest ever skid marks on a public road stretched for 951 feet (290 m) after an accident near Luton, England, in 1960.

▲ *Thrust SSC*, driven by Andy Green, holds the world land speed record. It is powered by two jet engines taken from fighter aircraft.

▶The world's largest tires are fitted to giant dumper trucks. They measure 14 feet (4.3 m) across and weigh 12,500 pounds (5,670 kg).

New York

◀ A 1931 Bugatti Type 41 Royale Sports Coupé was sold in 1990 for $15.7 million. Only six of these cars were ever made.

The most expensive car ever sold was a 1962 Ferrari 250 GTO. It fetched $34.65 million in 2014. A new Lamborghini Veneno Roadster costs $4.5 million.

Eco-Cars

very gasoline-powered car pollutes the air by pouring out poisonous exhaust gases. Burning one gallon (3.8 liters) of gasoline produces over 19 pounds (9 kg) of carbon dioxide, the chief cause of global warming. Scrapped cars contribute to vast amounts of environmental waste. In the 1990s, the state of California decided that a percentage of new cars must be "zero emission vehicles": they must not produce pollution. It is hoped that California's policy will be followed globally—the search is on for an "eco-car."

An efficient car travels a long distance for the amount of fuel it uses. An average family car in the United States does 26.4 miles per gallon of gasoline (8.9 liters per 100 km). Specially built three-wheelers can do 7,500 mpg (0.003 L/100 km).

▼ Up to 15 million cars are scrapped each year in the United States alone. Cars are the most recycled product in the United States, but much waste is still buried in landfill sites.

FACTFILE
TAKING UP SPACE
Every car requires more than 2,000 square feet (200 m²) of tarmac and concrete in the form of road and parking space.

FACTFILE
BUG POWER
In Brazil, many cars are powered with the help of bacteria. The cars run on gasohol, a mixture of gasoline and alcohol made by bacteria from sugar cane. Gasohol is cheaper than pure gasoline.

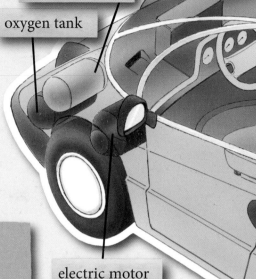

hydrogen tank

oxygen tank

electric motor

Low Pollution

Catalytic converter

platinum and other precious metals

► In the future, most of the material in a car will be reused. Plastics can be used to make plastic sheets. Metal parts can be used to make steel. Seat stuffing can be used as insulating material.

◄ The car of the future will use a fuel cell to produce electric power. The fuel cell uses hydrogen and oxygen to make electricity. The only waste product is water, which is non-polluting.

▼ The 1992 Renault Zoom made parking easy. It could shrink in size by folding the rear wheels forward.

glass

plastic

steel

accident warning beam

▼ Most cars now have a catalytic converter to remove harmful pollutants from the exhaust gases. Converters contain precious metals, such as platinum, which destroy the pollutants.

catalytic converter

FACTFILE
FILTHY CARS

In one year, the average passenger car produces:
- 9,737 pounds (4,417 kg) of carbon dioxide
- 248 pounds (112 kg) of carbon monoxide
- 18.32 pounds (8.3 kg) of nitrogen dioxide.

Car battery

▼ Batteries are an important component of pollution-free cars. They produce very little waste as nine-tenths of all batteries are recycled.

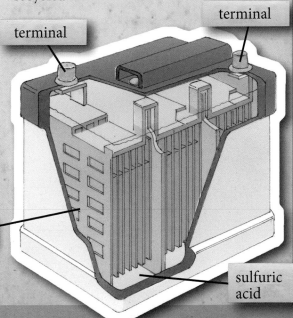

terminal

terminal

lead plate

sulfuric acid

Computer Cars

▼ Computer chips are thin wafers of silicon which contain all the parts of an electronic circuit. They are able to perform a great variety of tasks.

Computer chips are found in television sets, cameras, video games, office machines, spacecraft—and motor cars. These chips control the devices they are part of, ensuring they operate efficiently. Before long, in-car computers will be able to navigate and find the best route to a destination without the driver's help. The car of the future should make driving much easier and more enjoyable.

infrared beam

joystick control lever

windshield instrument display

navigation computer

generator

electric motor

▶ An in-car computer would constantly adjust the engine to reduce fuel consumption and adjust the suspension to suit road conditions. Normally, a driver controls steering and speed, but an infra-red beam could measure the proximity of other vehicles and if necessary, the computer could take control to avoid an accident.

batteries

computer-controlled suspension

▶ Roadside computers could control tightly packed "car trains" to maximize highway use.

28

▼ An in-car computer can acesss traffic information by a radio link with a control center. Incoming data from space satellites, called Global Positioning Satellites, can already pinpoint the car's location to within about 15 feet (4.5 m).

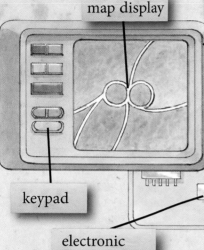

map display

receiver unit

keypad

electronic circuit board

battery

◀ Drivers could play chess or other games while traveling under computer control. The driver's opponent would be the car's computer.

▲ The computerized car would notify the police by radio if it is stolen. It could send out a radio signal for the police to follow, or transmit its position.

◢ Many cars have electronic control units with computer chips. These units monitor engine performance and adjust the engine to increase efficiency and reduce pollution.

FACTFILE
THE FUTURE IS HERE!

• By 2020, several manufacturers expect to be selling cars that can drive themselves at least part of the time.

• By 2040, it is estimated that 75 percent of cars will be self-driving.

Car Quiz

1. Approximately how many cars are there in the world today?
   a) 500 million
   b) 1 billion
   c) 1.5 billion

2. Who invented the four-stroke internal combustion engine?
   a) Karl Benz
   b) Nikolaus Otto
   c) Nicolas-Joseph Cugnot

3. Who made the first car to use a gasoline engine?
   a) Gottlieb Daimler
   b) Nikolaus Otto
   c) Karl Benz

4. How many different parts are there in an average motor car?
   a) 10,000
   b) 20,000
   c) 30,000

5. How long does a solar-powered car take to travel across Australia?
   a) About 6 days
   b) About 2 weeks
   c) About 1 month

6. What is the world's fastest production car?
   a) Bugatti Veyron Super Sport
   b) Lamborghini Diablo
   c) Lada 1200

7. What is the world's most expensive second-hand car?
   a) Mercedes CLK CTR
   b) Ferrari 250 GTO
   c) Bugatti Type 41 Royale

8. What is the world's best-selling car?
   a) Toyota Corolla
   b) Volkswagen Beetle
   c) Ford Model T

9. What is the fuel consumption of an average American car?
   a) 15 miles per gallon (15.7 liters per 100 km)
   b) 26.4 mpg (8.9 L/100 km)
   c) 35 mpg (6.7 L/100 km)

10. How many cars are scrapped in the United States each year?
    a) up to 5 million
    b) up to 10 million
    c) up to 15 million

Quiz answers

1) b   see page 7
2) b   see page 8
3) c   see page 8
4) c   see page 12
5) a   see page 19
6) a   see page 24
7) b   see page 25
8) a   see page 24
9) b   see page 26
10) c   see page 26

Glossary

acceleration
The rate at which speed changes with time. When a car's speed is increasing, it is accelerating.

air bag A large balloon which inflates quickly to protect the driver when a car crashes.

antilock brakes
Computer-controlled brakes that allow a car to be steered safely while braking.

battery A device that stores electrical energy. A car uses a battery to start the engine.

camshaft A shaft which, as it rotates, opens and closes the valves of an engine.

carburettor
A device that mixes air with a fine spray of fuel before it is fed into an internal combustion engine.

catalytic converter
A device fitted to the exhaust system of a car to eliminate harmful gases from the exhaust fumes.

chassis The strong metal frame to which the engine, body, and other parts of a car are attached.

computer chip
A set of miniature electronic circuits built on a small piece of silicon. It is sometimes called a silicon chip.

crankshaft A shaft in an engine that turns as the pistons go up and down.

diesel engine
An internal combustion engine which uses diesel oil as fuel.

differential
A device in the center of the rear axle of a car. It allows the back wheels to turn at different rates as the car turns, to prevent skidding.

disc brake A type of brake using a metal disc attached to the wheel. When the disc is pressed by pads, called brake pads, it is slowed. This in turn slows the wheel.

distributor
The part of the electrical system which passes (distributes) high-voltage electricity to the spark plugs.

four-stroke engine
An internal combustion engine in which the power is produced in four movements of the piston.

fuel injector
A device which squirts (injects) fuel into the cylinder of a diesel engine, when the air in the cylinder is compressed.

gearbox The part of the transmission system that passes the power of the engine to the propeller shaft.

generator A device that produces electrical energy when its central shaft, or rotor, is turned.

Global Positioning Satellite A satellite in orbit around the Earth, which enables the position of objects on Earth to be located.

internal combustion engine
An engine in which a fuel, such as gasoline or diesel oil, is burned inside the cylinders to produce power.

joystick A short lever that is used to control the movements of an aircraft or other machine.

km/h Kilometers per hour—a measurement of speed in the metric system.

photocell
A device that produces an electric current when light falls on it.

piston The part of an engine that moves up and down inside the cylinder.

pollution Harmful waste materials released into the environment.

rocket engine
A type of engine used in spacecraft. A stream of hot gases is expelled from the rear of the engine, driving the rocket forward.

roll bars Strong bars placed over and around a racing driver's seat, to protect the driver from injury if the car rolls over.

shock absorber
A device attached to the wheels of a car to reduce vibration on a bumpy road.

spark plug
A device connected to the cylinder of a gasoline engine that uses an electric spark to ignite the fuel–air mixture in the cylinder.

two-stroke engine
An internal combustion engine that produces its power with two movements of the piston.

valve A device that opens and closes to control the flow of gases and fuel into and out of an engine or other machine.

zero-emission vehicle A road vehicle that emits (gives out) no harmful exhaust gases.

Index